IS FOR
HARLEM

DINAH JOHNSON

ART BY **APRIL HARRISON**

Christy Ottaviano Books

LITTLE, BROWN AND COMPANY
New York   Boston

This book is dedicated to
Harlem's children, young and old—
those who call it home,
those who visit
&
those who hold Harlem
in their hearts.
—DJ

Langston Hughes once said,
"I was in love with Harlem long before I got there."
My sentiments exactly, so this book is quite simply
dedicated to Harlem with love.
—AH

ABOUT THIS BOOK

The illustrations for this book were done in mixed media/collage, acrylic, and artist pens on illustration board, and were photographed by Eli Warren. This book was edited by Christy Ottaviano and designed by Patrick Collins with art direction from Saho Fujii. The production was supervised by Nyamekye Waliyaya, and the production editor was Jen Graham. The text was set in Gill Sans.

Text copyright © 2022 by Dinah Johnson • Illustrations copyright © 2022 by April Harrison • Cover illustration copyright © 2022 by April Harrison • Cover design by Patrick Collins • Cover copyright © 2022 by Hachette Book Group, Inc. • Copyright credits for the rendered likenesses of artworks: M spread, from left to right: Romare Bearden, *Sunset and Moonrise with Maudell Sleet*, 1978. © Romare Bearden Foundation/ Licensed by VAGA at ARS, NY; © Jacob Lawrence, *The Migration Series, No. 58*, 1941; Alison Saar, *White Guise*, 2018. Wood, copper, ceiling tin, bronze, and tar. 91 x 40 x 30 in. © Alison Saar. Courtesy of L.A. Louver, Venice, CA; Kara Walker, *Emancipation Approximation, Scene #18*, 2000. Silkscreen. © Kara Walker, courtesy of Sikkema Jenkins & Co. and Sprüth Magers; © Lorna Simpson, *Easy For Who to Say*, 1989; © Hale Woodruff, *Picking Cotton*, 1926 (partial scene); *T* spread: Alison Saar, *Swing Low, Harriet Tubman Memorial*, 2007. Bronze. 156 x 180 x 96 in. Located at 122nd St. and St. Nicholas Ave., Harlem, New York. © Alison Saar. Courtesy of L.A. Louver, Venice, CA. • Hachette Book Group supports the right to free expression and the value of copyright. The purpose of copyright is to encourage writers and artists to produce the creative works that enrich our culture. • The scanning, uploading, and distribution of this book without permission is a theft of the author's intellectual property. If you would like permission to use material from the book (other than for review purposes), please contact permissions@hbgusa.com. Thank you for your support of the author's rights. • Christy Ottaviano Books • Hachette Book Group • 1290 Avenue of the Americas, New York, NY 10104 • Visit us at LBYR.com • First Edition: July 2022 • Christy Ottaviano Books is an imprint of Little, Brown and Company. • The Christy Ottaviano Books name and logo are trademarks of Hachette Book Group, Inc. • The publisher is not responsible for websites (or their content) that are not owned by the publisher. • Library of Congress Cataloging-in-Publication Data • Names: Johnson, Dinah, author. | Harrison, April, illustrator. • Title: H is for Harlem / words by Dinah Johnson ; art by April Harrison. • Description: First edition. | New York : Little, Brown and Company, [2022] | "Christy Ottaviano books." | Audience: Ages 5–9 | Summary: "A richly informative alphabet picture book celebrating Harlem's vibrant traditions, past and present." —Provided by publisher. • Identifiers: LCCN 2021010540 | ISBN 9780316322379 (hardcover) • Subjects: LCSH: African Americans—New York (State)—New York—History—Juvenile literature. | English language—Alphabet—Juvenile literature. | Harlem (New York, N.Y.)—History—Juvenile literature. • Classification: LCC F128.68.H3 J64 2022 | DDC 974.7/1—dc23 • LC record available at https://lccn.loc.gov/2021010540 • ISBN 978-0-316-32237-9 • PRINTED IN CHINA • APS • 10 9 8 7 6 5 4 3 2 1

A NOTE FROM THE AUTHOR

You probably know the names of many cities and communities that are important to American history. New York might be one of those places. This South Carolina girl—that's me—is fascinated with all of New York City's neighborhoods; each one is unique. But I wrote this book because I've spent so much time in Harlem that it feels like a second home. And because I'm a student of African American culture, I've read a lot about this special place. I want to share just a bit of what I've learned in *H Is for Harlem*.

Maybe you already know about the Harlem Renaissance, a period lasting from the 1910s through the mid-1930s, when Harlem was jumping with amazing energy. This energy has inspired countless individuals and organizations. In the 1940s, for example, the American Negro Theatre celebrated Black experiences on the stage. And over the years, talented orators such as Marcus Garvey have spoken powerful words that inspire us still. From 1979 to 1994, there was Lois Alexander Lane's Black Fashion Museum, whose collection now belongs to the National Museum of African American History and Culture. These are just a few of the stories connected to this incredible community.

Whether they know it or not, the people who live in Harlem are surrounded by the work of African American architect J. Max Bond Jr., whose vision had a lasting impact on buildings all around New York and especially in Harlem. The buildings are beautiful, and so are the children and grown-ups who lived and worked in them years ago and at this very moment in history. The energy, pride, and sense of purpose of its residents make Harlem just as exciting as ever. It is a place of possibility.

I hope that you read *H Is for Harlem* and learn a little about this dynamic, historic, wonderful neighborhood. And I hope you feel inspired to learn more, not only about Harlem but about the places where *you* live and the places that *you* love.

Dinah Johnson

IS FOR **APOLLO THEATER.**

In New York, it might be fun to ride the **A train**, the longest subway line in the city. Get off at the 125th Street station, in the heart of Harlem, and you can walk right over to the world-famous **Apollo Theater**. Don't forget to rub the lucky stone as you go in. If it's Wednesday, you can stay for the Amateur Night talent show. Maybe you've heard of Little Stevie Wonder, the Jackson 5, James Brown, or Aretha Franklin. Before becoming legendary musicians, they performed on the Apollo stage. Like those who inspired them, Usher, Jennifer Hudson, and other stars of today bring audiences to their feet.

 **IS FOR BOYS CHOIR OF HARLEM.**

On a special weekend each year, you can go to the **Harlem Book Fair**. There are books everywhere you look. Some of them were written by famous Harlem writers, like Langston Hughes and Zora Neale Hurston, alongside those written by powerful authors of today. Luckily, you don't have to wait for a special weekend to watch videos of the **Boys Choir of Harlem and the Girls Choir of Harlem**, sometimes together, pouring their hearts into every single note. Whether singing the blues or spirituals, jazz or pop, they will surely make your heart soar.

IS FOR **HARLEM CHILDREN'S ZONE.**

There are many organizations in Harlem that cherish children and work hard on their behalf, turning that love into action. One such organization is **Harlem Children's Zone**, founded by Geoffrey Canada. HCZ works hard to ensure that young people and families in Harlem have the education, the health care, the knowledge, and the tools that make it possible for them to achieve their dreams.

IS FOR DANCE THEATRE OF HARLEM.

The night after Martin Luther King Jr. was killed in 1968, choreographer Arthur Mitchell called his friends, actors Cicely Tyson and Brock Peters, to meet at his home to brainstorm ways to honor Dr. King's memory. This meeting inspired the creation of the **Dance Theatre of Harlem** in 1969 by Mitchell and ballet mentor Karel Shook. Since then, the Dance Theatre of Harlem has been training young people to make magic with their bodies. The dancers represent Harlem with grace and power and energy in every city they visit—all around the world. Every step they dance is beautiful and bold.

 **IS FOR EDGECOMBE AVENUE.**

For a long time, **409 Edgecombe Avenue** was the tallest building in Harlem. It was home to Thurgood Marshall, the first African American US Supreme Court justice; Aaron Douglas, painter extraordinaire; and W. E. B. Du Bois, coeditor, along with the fabulous Jessie Fauset, of the *The Brownies' Book*, a magazine for children published from 1920 to 1921. Can you imagine the interesting and important things people talked about in this building on Edgecombe Avenue?

IS FOR **FIGURE SKATING IN HARLEM.**

Mabel **Fairbanks** spent some of her childhood in Harlem and Midtown Manhattan, where she was enthralled watching white people ice-skating at Central Park. Against enormous odds, she became a skater and coach and in 1997 was inducted into the US Figure Skating Hall of Fame. That same year, Sharon Cohen founded **Figure Skating in Harlem**, which helps girls honor their bodies and their minds through skating and friendship. The girls learn to "glide into their power," believing that they can accomplish anything they set their minds to.

G IS FOR **HARLEM GLOBETROTTERS.**

Some basketball fans might know about the Harlem Rens, who played from 1923 until 1949. They were fabulous pioneers in their field. But almost everybody has heard about the **Harlem Globetrotters**, ambassadors for Harlem, USA, all around the world. Since 1926, they have played like no other team ever. They do a four-point shot, the figure-eight weave, fast breaks, and slam dunks while the crowds cheer at the top of their lungs. Go, Globetrotters!

IS FOR **HARLEM**.

Harlem is a place like no other in the world. The Lenape, an American Indian people, were the first to live here and to honor this land they called Muscota.

In the 1600s, immigrants arrived from the Netherlands and named it after a city called Haarlem, spelled with a double letter A. Harlem has been home to many Americans, with ancestors from many countries. It is truly multicultural. But for a long time people have called Harlem the mecca of Black America, a place where African American culture is living and breathing, shining and indestructible.

IS FOR **IMPACT FARM.**

Impact Farm and Harlem Grown are groups that help children learn about urban farming, nutrition, and sustainability. *Urban* means "in the city." *Nutrition* means how we feed our bodies. *Sustainability* means how to use the earth's resources wisely. Impact Farm is actually made up of many different locations that were once abandoned and are now beautiful and fruitful because of their work. They also have greenhouses and gardens at schools—where seeds are planted not only in the ground but in the minds and hearts of Harlem's children.

J IS FOR **NATIONAL JAZZ MUSEUM IN HARLEM.**

At the **National Jazz Museum in Harlem**, you can learn about Louis Armstrong, Ella Fitzgerald, and many other musicians who created music that still makes people hum and snap their fingers. If your teachers or parents take you there, you might hear today's greats, like Wynton Marsalis and Geri Allen. You can sing scat, and dance, and even hang out at a petting zoo of instruments—the instruments that musicians play to make jazzy Harlem jazz!

THE
NATIONAL
JAZZ
MUSEUM
IN
HARLEM

 **IS FOR KINFOLK.**

Early in the twentieth century, during the Great Migration, thousands of people from southern states made new homes up north. Many of them were leaving behind their **kinfolk**—another word for family—hoping to start brand-new lives. So today, when people from down south head to New York, many of them have kinfolk waiting with arms open wide, ready to show them the sights and sounds of Harlem.

IS FOR **LIBERATION BOOKSTORE.**

Liberation Bookstore, Hue-Man Bookstore, and Lewis H. Michaux's National Memorial African Bookstore are an important part of the story of Harlem. Over the years, they have sold books about Black history and politics, art and astronomy, architecture and dance, and so much more. Some people are lucky enough to own books their parents or grandparents bought at the beloved Liberation Bookstore.

IS FOR STUDIO MUSEUM IN HARLEM.

At the **Studio Museum in Harlem**, you can see tens of thousands of photographs and paintings, sculptures and installations, and pieces of art you've never imagined. You'll learn names like Bearden and Lawrence, Saar and Simpson, Walker and Woodruff. The museum is a dynamic, daring, busy, beautiful celebration of art by artists beloved in Harlem, in America, and in countries all around the world.

AMNESIA   ERROR   INDIFFERENCE   OMISSION   UNCIVIL

STUDIO
MUSEUM
HARLEM

 **IS FOR NEW YORK CITY.**

New York City is home to magical buildings like the Empire State Building. It is home to gleaming streets like Broadway. It is home to marvelous neighborhoods like Chinatown and Chelsea, Spanish Harlem and Washington Heights. It is home to boroughs like Brooklyn and the Bronx, Queens, and Staten Island. But New York City would not be New York City without Harlem!

IS FOR *OPPORTUNITY* MAGAZINE.

Opportunity: A Journal of Negro Life, and *The Crisis*, and *The Brownies' Book*, too, are important magazines in the history of Harlem. You can find all of them at the Library of Congress in Washington, DC, in person or online. If you want to get a peek into the lives of Black children and their parents who lived in Harlem long ago, just look through the pages of these magazines and you might see a face that reminds you of you!

The Brownies' Book

JANUARY, 1920

OPPORTUNITY
A JOURNAL OF NEGRO LIFE

CRISIS

P IS FOR **PHOTOGRAPHERS.**

For decades, James VanDerZee and Austin Hansen took extraordinary **photographs**. Somehow, it seems that one of them was always on the scene with his camera when something big, or just ordinary, was happening in Harlem. Thousands of Hansen's pictures, VanDerZee's pictures, and those of many other talented photographers are waiting for your eyes at the Schomburg Center for Research in Black Culture.

IS FOR **HARLEM QUARTET.**

Quartet means "four"—so **Harlem Quartet** is a group of four musicians. They play string instruments—violin, viola, and cello. The members of the group take the classical music of Europe and flavor it with jazz. President Barack Obama and First Lady Michelle Obama hosted Harlem Quartet at the White House. Their recording "Mozart Goes Dancing" won a Grammy Award. That's a big deal! Harlem Quartet takes their music all around the world, celebrating Harlem and the musical artists of the Harlem Renaissance.

IS FOR **RESTAURANTS.**

The **Red Rooster restaurant** is a favorite Harlem gathering place, just like the first Red Rooster that it honors. And for decades, Sylvia's has been legendary. You can't miss their Sunday gospel brunch! Sylvia's and Red Rooster are both restaurants where people from different neighborhoods and nations get together to eat and talk and laugh, listen to music, and look at the amazing photographs and art on the walls. At Sylvia's, the food has a little taste of South Carolina. At Red Rooster, you can find food with a little taste of Sweden or Ethiopia. And these restaurants always have the flavor of Harlem!

IS FOR SCHOMBURG.

S is an important letter in Harlem. There is **Strivers' Row**, where many fascinating people have lived. There's the **Savoy Ballroom**, which was always jumping with music and dance. And you should definitely visit the

Sugar Hill Children's Museum of Art & Storytelling.

The most magnificent *S* of all is the **Schomburg Center for Research in Black Culture**. The New York Public Library acquired Arturo Alfonso Schomburg's impressive collection of books, pamphlets, and art in 1926. And Schomburg himself served as the curator from 1932 until his death in 1938. The division was renamed in his honor in 1940. Arturo Schomburg was a true bibliophile, a person who loves books. The books closest to his heart were those that teach readers about life in the African diaspora—everywhere that people of African descent have called home.

T IS FOR **HARRIET TUBMAN.**

The **Harriet Tubman Memorial** is a sculpture by artist Alison Saar, honoring the most important conductor of the Underground Railroad. Saar calls her creation *Swing Low*—like the words in the famous spiritual about God's chariot swinging low so that enslaved people could get on board and make their way to freedom. The Tubman statue is thirteen feet tall, majestic like Tubman, and facing south, reminding us that Harriet Tubman was always thinking about the people she led from south to north, from slavery to freedom.

U IS FOR UPTOWN.

When some people say **Uptown**, they mean any street north of 59th Street. Others mean Harlem, from 110th Street way up to 155th Street. Artist Bryan Collier created a beautiful book called *Uptown*—a celebration of the sights and sounds, the rhythms and voices of this special neighborhood. His book is a Harlem, Uptown love song.

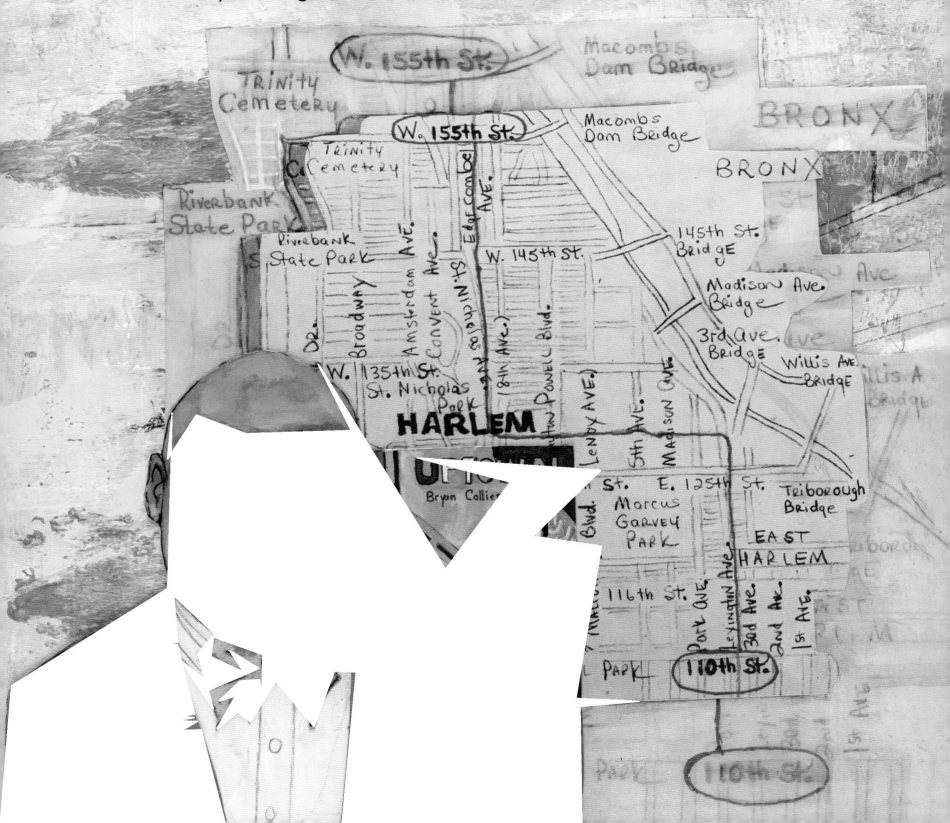

IS FOR **VOICES.**

You can hear the **voices** of Harlem as you walk down streets that are humming with history. You can hear the voices of Harlem praying in Abyssinian Baptist Church. You can hear them in hospitals, in living rooms, and bursting from books. Voices laughing and debating, remembering, and planning for the future. You can hear voices from Port-au-Prince, Haiti, and Charleston, South Carolina; from Paris, France, and Accra, Ghana; from Brooklyn, New York, or around the corner. You can hear the voices of Harlem's children everywhere.

Abyssinian Baptist Church
132 Odell Clark Place

W IS FOR MADAM C. J. WALKER.

Years ago, lots of people depended on popular hair care and beauty products made and sold by **Madam C. J. Walker**. She was one of the first American women to become a millionaire not because her parents were rich but because she was smart and worked hard. She had heart. Harlem was one of the places that she called home. Madam Walker was a philanthropist. That means she used her money to do good things for many people and many causes, in many places, including Harlem.

X IS FOR MALCOLM X BOULEVARD.

Malcolm X was born in Omaha, Nebraska, but he adopted Harlem and Harlem adopted him. He fought with all his heart for Black people there and across America to be able to live freely and in peace. You can read his powerful words in his autobiography, his life story. When you're in Harlem, remember that Lenox Avenue is the same as **Malcolm X Boulevard**, a street so important that it has two names! Busy people walking this beautiful street are never too busy to remember Malcolm X.

"THE FUTURE BELONGS TO THOSE WHO PREPARE FOR IT TODAY.
— MALCOLM X

IS FOR **HARLEM YMCA**.

The Harlem branch of the YMCA was built during a time when African Americans were not welcome at the other branches. But the **Harlem YMCA** was jumping with performers, like Eartha Kitt, and visitors, like baseball legend Jackie Robinson, pioneering scientist George Washington Carver, and writer Claude McKay. The work of African American artists graces its walls. Aaron Douglas's mural *Evolution of Negro Dance* is just one notable example. The Harlem YMCA is so special that in 1976 it was named a National Historic Landmark.

"If a man is not faithful to his own individuality, he cannot be loyal to anything."

–Claude McKay

IS FOR ZORA NEALE HURSTON.

Zora Neale Hurston was a native of Florida, but she is central to any history of Harlem. By some accounts, she was the first African American to debut a Broadway play—*The Great Day*. She was not only a playwright but an anthropologist, too, which means she studied why people live how they do. And she was a novelist and a folklorist, someone who studies what people believe and records the stories that people tell. Zora Neale Hurston loved to tell big stories to the other writers, artists, and thinkers who often gathered at her home. These Harlemites paved the way for the Harlem of today!

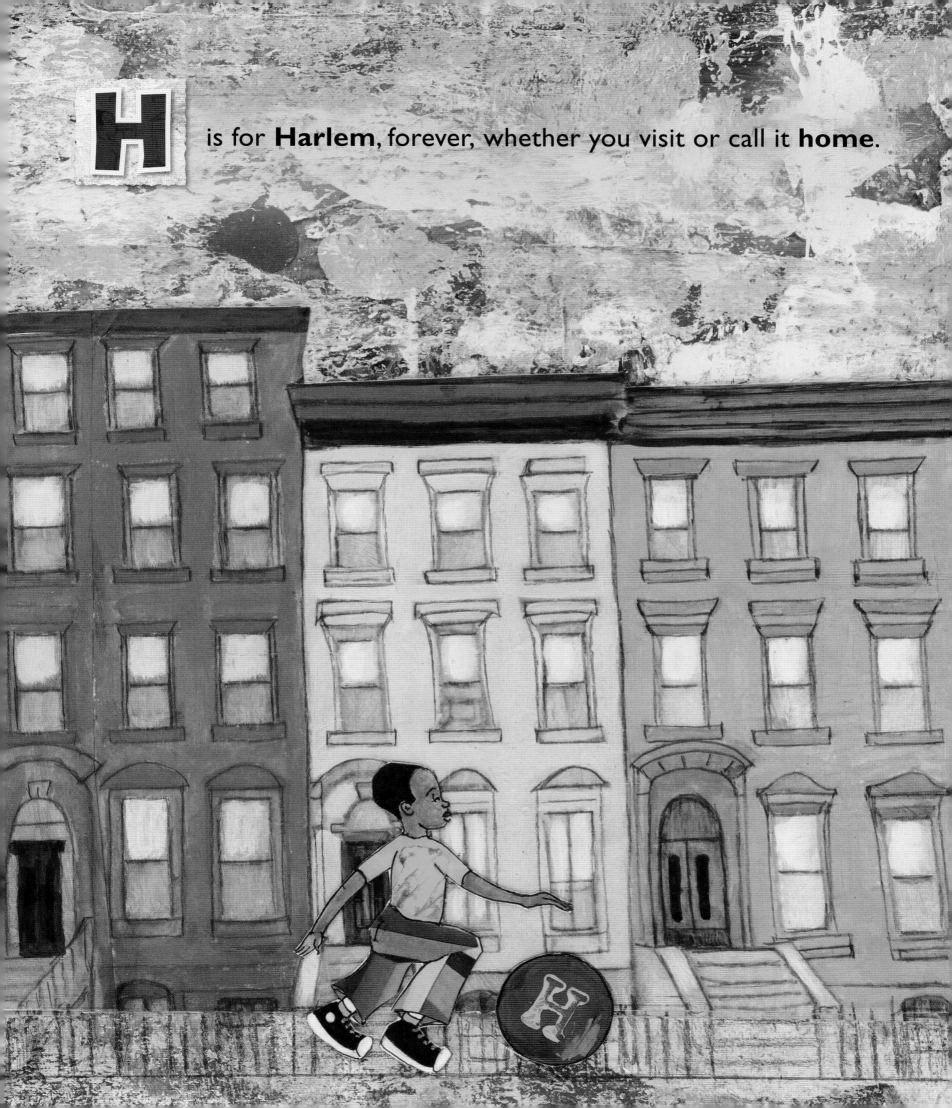

H is for **Harlem**, forever, whether you visit or call it **home**.